ENVIRONMENT

MICHAEL ALLABY

award

Series editor: Elizabeth Miles
Cover design: Duck Egg Blue
Illustrations: Mike Saunders, Jim Channell, Gary Hincks,
Ruth Lindsay, Brian Pearce, David Wright and Julian Baker
Photography: Shutterstock.com (Deni_Sugandi, Gecko1968, Vadim Orlov, Anna Kucherova pchais,
EvrenKalinbacak, Jag_cz, nouseforname, Stephane Bidouze, apstockphoto, Liv Oeian, Bernhard Staehli,
Dmitri Mikitenko, Karel Bartik, Helena81, Juergen_Wallstabe, Alex van Schaik, Heinz-Peter Schwerin, nwdph,
Golubev Dmitrii, Henrik Larsson, Jemny, Ondris, Janelle Lugge, Tarpan, Joe Morris 917, Andy Heyward,
D. Kucharski K. Kucharska, PHOTO FUN, Mark robert paton, Pinosub, ipsener, Costin Constantinescu,
FloridaStock, Viesturs Ozolins, hanohiki, Christiane Schwerin); NASA, NASA Goddard/Katy Mersmann

ISBN 978-1-78270-003-6

This edition first published 2022

Published by Award Publications Limited,
The Old Riding School, Welbeck,
Worksop, S80 3LR

 /awardpublications @award.books @award_books
www.awardpublications.co.uk

21-984 1

Printed in China

Contents

What is the Environment?

We can think of the whole of Planet Earth as the environment. An environment is a place in which living things can find food and shelter. It consists of the surroundings (the rocks, soil, air and water) and the living things themselves. On Earth, life is possible almost everywhere. Scientists study detailed aspects of the environment, but all these aspects are linked, so what affects one part of the environment may also affect others.

Nowadays, people know that if they protect the air, water, plants and animals close to where they live, they are also helping to protect the global environment. Many people are anxious to reduce pollution, too, so that the environment is better for people as well as for wildlife.

Planet Earth

The environment that surrounds us is tiny compared to the depth of the Earth beneath. The Earth is formed in layers. The inner layers are very hot and around 1,000–2,000 kilometres thick. At the centre of the Earth, the inner core is made of hot, solid metal. This is covered by the outer core, a layer of molten metal. Around the outer core are the inner and outer mantles made of semi-molten rock. The soil and rock on which we live are called the crust – a layer only 5–60 kilometres thick. Above this, the atmosphere forms a thin outer covering around the Earth.

The crust is made of large plates that move, causing cracks, ridges and mountains

The outer mantle also contains molten rock, which sometimes erupts from volcanoes

Nearly 9 kilometres high, Mount Everest just reaches the stratosphere

The environment stretches from the bottom of the oceans to the top of the troposphere

The outer core is very hot – the temperature is over 5,000°C

The ozone layer is about 25 kilometres above the Earth's surface – it protects us from the Sun's rays

The atmosphere

The Earth's atmosphere can be divided into layers. The weather and most of the Earth's air are in the thinnest layer, called the troposphere (**1**). Above, in the stratosphere (**2**) lies the ozone gas that protects us from the Sun's harmful rays. Beyond are the mesosphere (**3**) and the thermosphere (**4**). The exosphere (**5**) rises to about 700 kilometres, where it merges with the Sun's atmosphere.

In the troposphere, clouds form and the Earth's weather occurs

Spectacular light displays called aurora sometimes appear in the thermosphere

Meteors burn up in the mesosphere

Plants and animals cannot live in the thin air of the stratosphere

5

300 km

4

80 km

3

50 km

2

12 km

1

0 km

Air and Water

Air and water change the environment. Along with sunshine, they affect climate, the weather and the type of vegetation that grows. At the Equator, the Sun is almost directly overhead at noon, so places on and near the Equator are warmed more strongly than elsewhere. When heated, the air moves away from the Equator. At the same time, cooler air moves towards the Equator. This circulation of the air brings us weather. The Earth's winds are a part of this air circulation. Ocean waters, in warm or cold currents, also affect climates because air is warmed or cooled as it passes over them.

Climate

Climate is the range of weather conditions found in a particular area. Generally, the further you go from the Equator, the colder the climate becomes. The climate of a region affects the type of vegetation found there. Rainforests (1) grow near the Equator, where the climate is hot and wet. Deserts (2) are in dry climates. Temperate forests (3) grow in mild climates, while evergreen forests (4) are often found in colder climates. In polar regions (5) there is little vegetation because the climate is dry and very cold.

South Pole

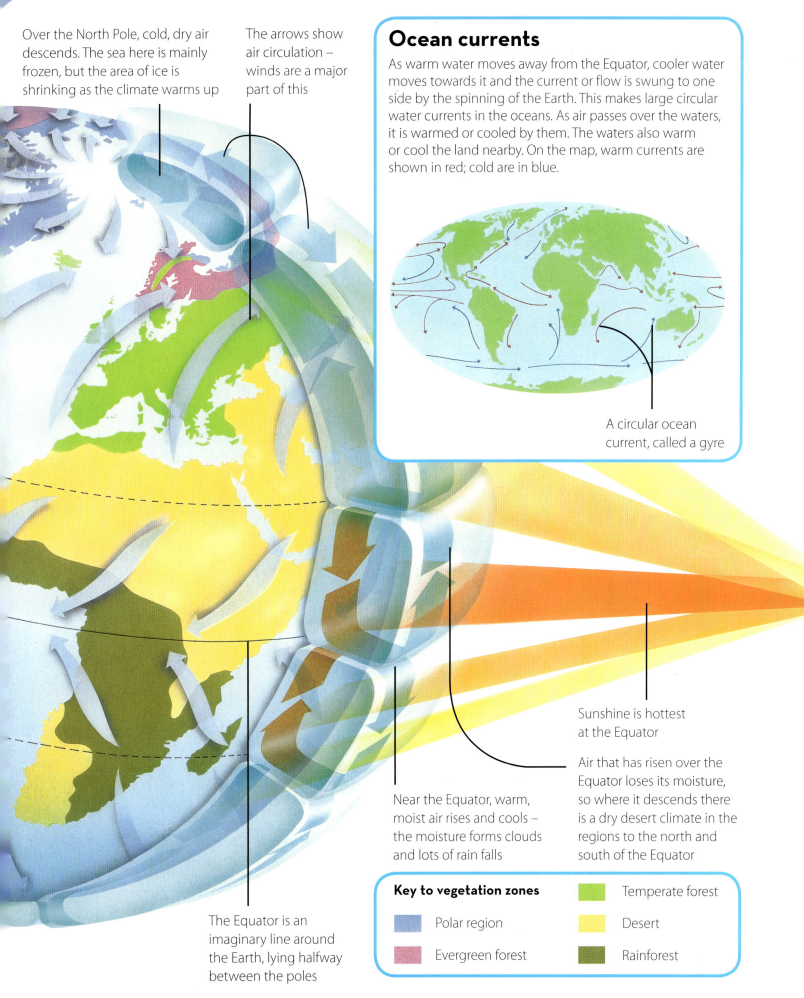

Over the North Pole, cold, dry air descends. The sea here is mainly frozen, but the area of ice is shrinking as the climate warms up

The arrows show air circulation – winds are a major part of this

Ocean currents

As warm water moves away from the Equator, cooler water moves towards it and the current or flow is swung to one side by the spinning of the Earth. This makes large circular water currents in the oceans. As air passes over the waters, it is warmed or cooled by them. The waters also warm or cool the land nearby. On the map, warm currents are shown in red; cold are in blue.

A circular ocean current, called a gyre

Sunshine is hottest at the Equator

Air that has risen over the Equator loses its moisture, so where it descends there is a dry desert climate in the regions to the north and south of the Equator

Near the Equator, warm, moist air rises and cools – the moisture forms clouds and lots of rain falls

The Equator is an imaginary line around the Earth, lying halfway between the poles

Key to vegetation zones

Polar region	Temperate forest
Evergreen forest	Desert
	Rainforest

The Ozone Layer

Sunlight, which we see as white, is really a mixture of the colours in a rainbow. The Sun also radiates light that we cannot see, some of it is called ultraviolet (UV) light.

If too much UV light reaches the Earth's surface, it is harmful and can cause skin cancer. However, a layer of ozone gas in the atmosphere protects us by absorbing some of the UV light. But in some parts of the world, particularly over Antarctica, the ozone layer has become thinner, allowing more UV light to reach the Earth.

The ozone layer, where ozone gathers, is 20–25 kilometres above the ground

As it passes through the ozone layer, some UV light is absorbed by ozone

A thinning of the ozone layer is sometimes described as an ozone hole

Where the ozone layer is thin, more UV light reaches the ground

Too much UV light causes sunburn and skin cancer

Ozone breakdown

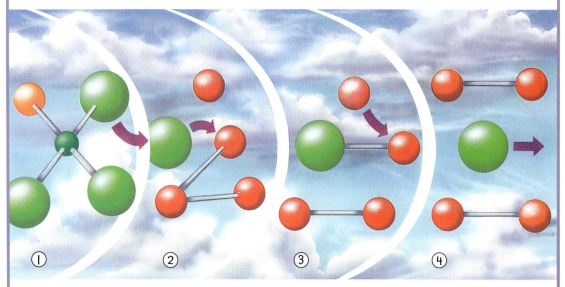

① ② ③ ④

In the ozone layer, there are gases that have chlorine atoms in their molecules. These gases include CFCs (chlorofluorocarbons). A CFC molecule with its chlorine atoms is pictured above (**I**). The chlorine atoms are shown in green. UV light from the Sun breaks these CFC molecules up and the chlorine atoms break off and float away. In winter over Antarctica, fierce winds blow around a centre of still air. As winter draws to an end, clouds of ice crystals form in the still air. On the surface of these crystals, the free chlorine atoms join up with ozone molecules (**2**). This removes an oxygen atom (red) from the ozone molecule and breaks up the molecule. The spare oxygen atom then leaves the chlorine to join another spare oxygen atom (**3**). The chlorine is then free to break down another ozone molecule (**4**). This reduces the amount of ozone in the ozone layer, making an ozone 'hole'. CFCs used to be widely used – in aerosol cans and refrigerators, for example. Once scientists discovered that these chemicals destroy ozone, their use was phased out.

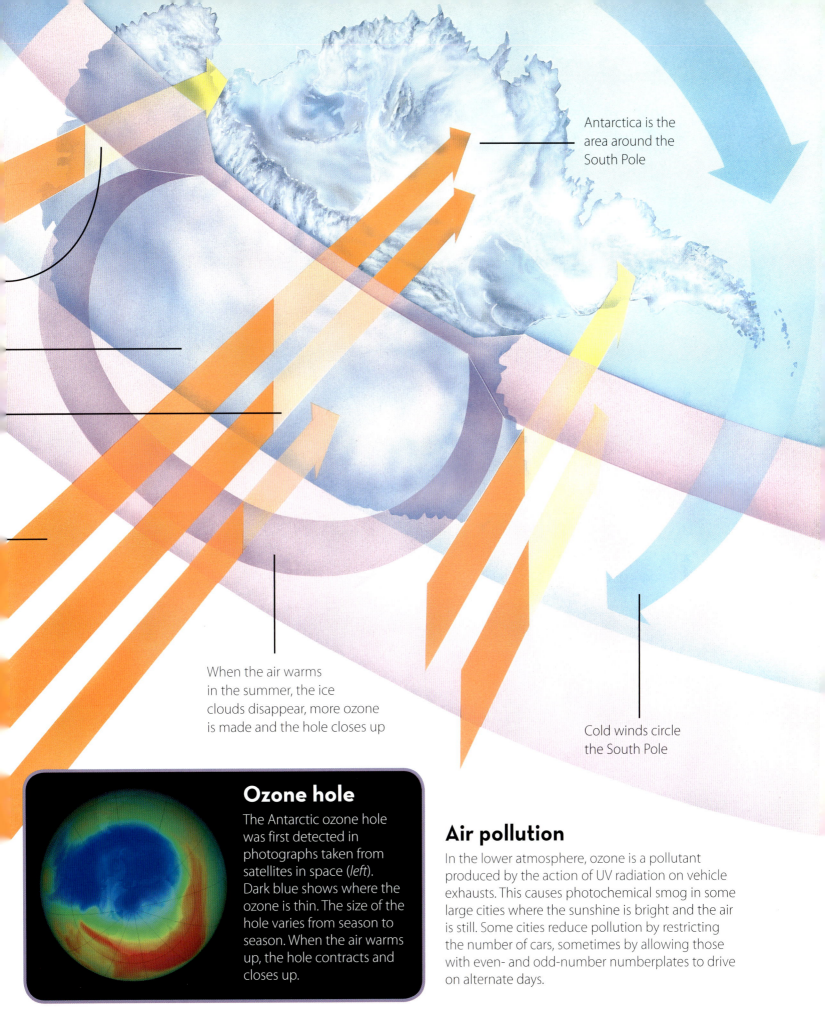

Antarctica is the
area around the
South Pole

When the air warms
in the summer, the ice
clouds disappear, more ozone
is made and the hole closes up

Cold winds circle
the South Pole

Ozone hole

The Antarctic ozone hole
was first detected in
photographs taken from
satellites in space (*left*).
Dark blue shows where the
ozone is thin. The size of the
hole varies from season to
season. When the air warms
up, the hole contracts and
closes up.

Air pollution

In the lower atmosphere, ozone is a pollutant
produced by the action of UV radiation on vehicle
exhausts. This causes photochemical smog in some
large cities where the sunshine is bright and the air
is still. Some cities reduce pollution by restricting
the number of cars, sometimes by allowing those
with even- and odd-number numberplates to drive
on alternate days.

The Greenhouse Effect

When the Sun's rays reach the ground or sea, they warm these surfaces, which then send heat back up into the atmosphere, warming some of the gases in the air. These 'greenhouse' gases are like a blanket, holding in heat that would otherwise escape into space. This is called the 'greenhouse effect' because, like the glass of a greenhouse, the gases allow energy to pass more easily inwards than outwards. Without it, the average temperature on Earth would be much colder, around -18°C instead of 15°C. But human activity and industrial processes are generating more greenhouse gases, which is upsetting the balance, causing our planet to heat up.

School strikes

Since it was begun in 2018 by schoolgirl activist Greta Thunberg, the School Strike for Climate movement has grown from just one person in Sweden to global demonstrations involving millions of protesters who take time out of school lessons on Fridays to demand action to tackle climate change.

Power stations burning coal or natural gas emit greenhouse gases

Carbon dioxide is the main greenhouse gas

Most climate scientists agree that the release of greenhouse gases must be reduced, as the global climate is already showing signs of getting warmer

Cars running on fossil fuels release carbon dioxide as well as nitrogen oxides. These affect air quality, and are harmful to the health of people and animals

The oceans store more than a third of the carbon dioxide we emit (*see pages 14–15*)

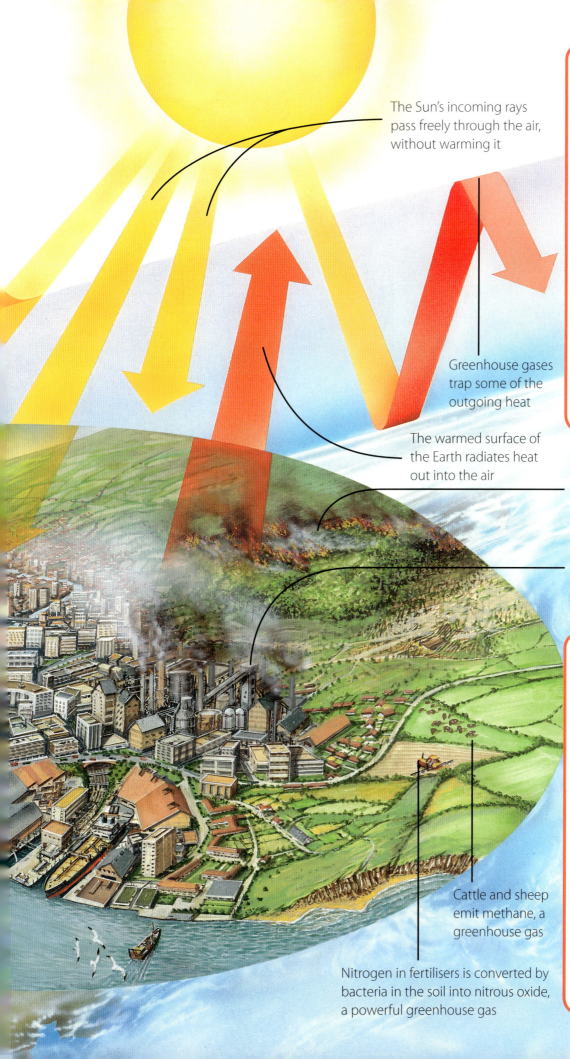

The Sun's incoming rays pass freely through the air, without warming it

Greenhouse gases trap some of the outgoing heat

The warmed surface of the Earth radiates heat out into the air

Cattle and sheep emit methane, a greenhouse gas

Nitrogen in fertilisers is converted by bacteria in the soil into nitrous oxide, a powerful greenhouse gas

Reducing greenhouse gases

Climate scientists and many governments want to reduce greenhouse gas emissions to lessen their warming effect. This is what the United Nations Paris Agreement set out to do by setting legally binding emission limits. Others believe that more efficient industry, capturing and burying carbon dioxide, and technologies such as alternative fuels, renewable energy sources and electric vehicles will solve the problem.

Burning trees – whether caused by wild fires or by forest clearing – release carbon dioxide

Greenhouse gases are also released by fossil-fueled power stations, factories and vehicles

Carbon footprint

Producing, processing and transporting all the food and other items we use releases carbon dioxide into the atmosphere. We cause the release of carbon dioxide when we travel in vehicles that burn petrol or diesel and when we use gas, electricity or coal at home. Measured as the amount of carbon dioxide produced, the impact that we each have on the environment is called our 'carbon footprint'. A smaller carbon footprint will affect the environment less than a larger one.

Gaia, the Living Earth

Every living organism alters the chemistry of its environment. Each time we breathe, we remove a little oxygen from the air and add a little carbon dioxide. After digesting food, our body rids itself of waste. Both alter the environment around us.

In 1979, a British scientist, James Lovelock, proposed the Gaia theory. On a 'living' planet, organisms alter their environment, managing or regulating it. In this way, said Lovelock, the Earth regulates itself, making sure there is enough oxygen for animals and carbon dioxide for plants, for example. Shown here is the way in which tiny marine plants and shellfish regulate the Earth's temperature and the amount of carbon dioxide (CO_2) in the air.

Carbon dioxide

Carbon dioxide is a greenhouse gas (*see pages 12–13*). It dissolves in rain and enters the sea. There, tiny plants and animals use it to make their shells of calcium carbonate. When the organisms die, their shells fall to the seabed. Eventually, these are ground down and form chalk and limestone rocks. Such rocks are very common and often contain fossils of the shells. This process removes some carbon dioxide from the air, but it takes many, many years to do so.

The average temperature on Earth has long been about 15°C, but most scientists now believe that climate change is causing the planet to warm up. Much of this extra heat is absorbed by the oceans, causing more storms and melting polar ice. That makes sea levels rise, threatening some islands and coastal communities.

Chalk cliffs were formed over millions of years by the build-up of dead marine organisms

Chalk cliffs are like giant storehouses for CO_2, stored as calcium carbonate

As dead shellfish and tiny organisms die and break up, some carbon dioxide (CO_2) is released

When sea organisms die, their bones and shells make a chalky sediment

The sediment becomes chalk or limestone rock, which will eventually be forced up to the surface of the sea

CO$_2$ dissolves in rain, which flows into rivers and then to the sea

Sulphur is released as marine organisms grow – this results in more clouds and makes temperatures fall

Sea organisms use CO$_2$ to make their bones and shells

Microscopic plants (called phytoplankton) give the sea a creamy appearance because of their chalky shells

Under a microscope, the fossils of tiny marine plants and shells can be seen in chalk

Tiny marine plants with chalky plates (seen under a microscope with other organisms)

Not too hot, not too cold

In the oceans, there are microscopic plant organisms that protect themselves with chalky plates, or shells. To make their shells, they use the greenhouse gas carbon dioxide (CO$_2$). The tiny plants also release a gaseous sulphur compound. This gas helps to make most of the clouds we see over oceans. Together, these processes help to regulate the Earth's temperature.

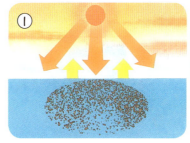 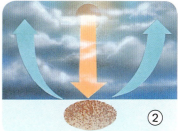

When skies are clear, the Sun's rays warm the Earth and its waters. The ocean's tiny plants then multiply faster and remove more CO$_2$ from the air. The multiplying plants also release more sulphur, which makes clouds form, cooling the ocean surface (1). As the water temperature cools, the tiny plants begin to die and as they decompose they release CO$_2$ back into the air (2). The amount of sulphur is reduced, the skies clear, the ocean warms up and the cycle begins again.

Plant Life

Plants are among the few living things on Earth that can make their own food. They do this through a process called photosynthesis. Sunlight falling on the plant's leaves is captured by chlorophyll, the substance in the cells that gives the plant its green colour. Energy from sunlight is used to combine water and carbon dioxide to make food in the form of sugars. This food is then transported to all the other parts of the plant, providing the energy it needs to live and grow.

Plants also use energy in taking the minerals they need from the soil to build their cells. The byproduct of photosynthesis is oxygen, which passes out of the plant and into the atmosphere through its leaves.

Sunlight falls on plant leaves

Chlorophyll captures the sunlight

During photosynthesis, oxygen is released into the atmosphere

Leaves are green because they contain chlorophyll

Water travels up vessels in the stem

Water and nutrients taken up from the soil enter through the roots

16

Carbon dioxide from the atmosphere enters through stomata in the leaf

Carbon dioxide, oxygen and water vapour pass through stomata

Respiration

Like animals, all plants continuously respire. Respiration is almost the reverse of photosynthesis: oxygen is taken in and carbon dioxide is released. The oxygen is used to break down the sugars the plant has made to produce the energy it needs to live.

During the day, photosynthesis occurs faster than respiration, so more carbon dioxide is taken in than released. At night, photosynthesis stops and carbon dioxide is not taken in; it is only released through respiration.

At night, only carbon dioxide and water vapour are released

The palisade layer

Water travels through these tubes

Photosynthesis takes place in chlorophyll inside the cylindrical cells

Sugars are stored in the mesophyll layer

Inside the leaf

This high-magnification cross-section of a leaf shows the cells where photosynthesis takes place. Water vapour, oxygen and carbon dioxide enter and leave through tiny holes (called stomata) found mainly on the lower surface of the leaf. Sunlight is absorbed by cylindrical cells in the palisade layer. The sugars made are then stored in the spongy mesophyll layer beneath, before being transported to other parts of the plant.

17

Food Webs

Most plants make their own food (*see pages 16–17*). They are the first in a line of organisms along which food-energy is passed. This line is called a 'food chain'. Plants, the 'primary producers', are the first link in the chain. The second link is plant-eating animals, called 'primary consumers'. Animals that eat other animals (meat eaters) are next. They are called 'secondary consumers'.

In a community of plants and animals, there are lots of food chains and many are connected. When two or more food chains are connected, they create a 'food web', like the one shown here (*right*).

Food chains

Most food chains begin with green plants. Plant eaters, such as rabbits, eat the plants. Digesting their food, moving and keeping warm or cool uses up nine tenths of the energy in the food. So a meat eater, such as a fox, gets only one tenth of the food energy eaten by a rabbit. This energy loss can be shown as a pyramid.

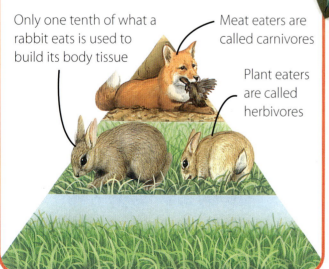

Only one tenth of what a rabbit eats is used to build its body tissue

Meat eaters are called carnivores

Plant eaters are called herbivores

Food webs are complex – this is a simplified food web of the African savannah grasslands

With their strong jaws and teeth, hyenas can crush large bones

Vultures are scavengers, feeding on the remains left behind by the hunters

The martial eagle hunts mammals and large birds

Grey crowned crane

A bee-eater

The banded mongoose eats plants and meat – it is an omnivore

Baboons feed on plants, insects, eggs, small birds, reptiles and mammals

The cheetah is a hunter – it can outrun a gazelle or antelope over a short distance

The leopard, a carnivore, eats meat of any kind

Giraffes can reach leaves on the highest branches of the acacia tree

Ants raid termite mounds

Termites build mounds and grow fungus to feed on

Compound stomachs allow impalas to digest grass

With its long, sticky tongue, the aardvark collects termites to eat

Living Oceans

Food chains in the oceans, like food chains on land, begin with photosynthesis in green plants. Most plants in the sea are microscopically small, but there are so many of them that they sometimes colour the water. These tiny plants float within 150 metres of the surface, where there is enough sunlight for photosynthesis to occur. Waste and dead organisms sink slowly from this sunlit zone, providing food for animals living in the twilight zone below. No light reaches deeper than about 180 metres and there is less food available, but some animals survive even at these depths.

Lantern fish are fairly common in the twilight zone

Food particles fall like rain towards the sea floor

Tripod-fish prop themselves up on their fins to feed on falling particles

Deep-sea vents

At vents in the ocean floor, hot water containing hydrogen sulphide is released. This chemical supports a special food chain of bacteria, worms and fish at depths where there is no sunlight and no photosynthesis.

Animals such as these sea cucumbers and worms live in ocean trenches, up to 10 kilometres below the surface

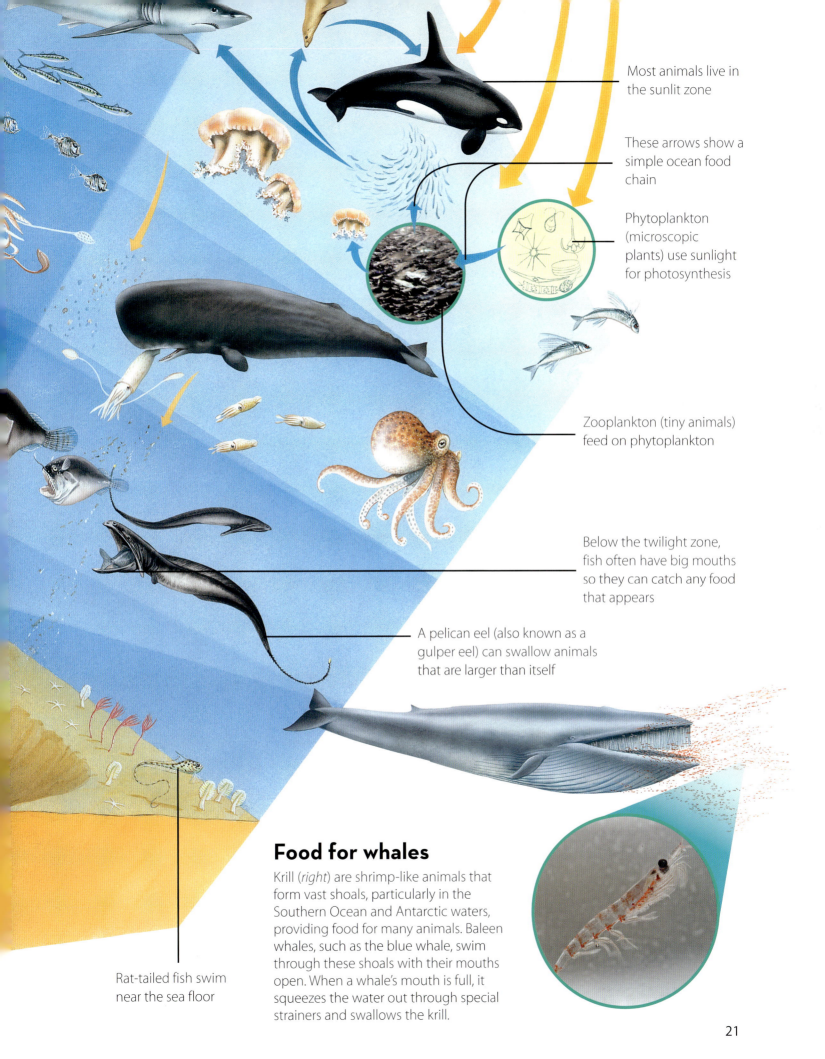

Most animals live in the sunlit zone

These arrows show a simple ocean food chain

Phytoplankton (microscopic plants) use sunlight for photosynthesis

Zooplankton (tiny animals) feed on phytoplankton

Below the twilight zone, fish often have big mouths so they can catch any food that appears

A pelican eel (also known as a gulper eel) can swallow animals that are larger than itself

Rat-tailed fish swim near the sea floor

Food for whales

Krill (*right*) are shrimp-like animals that form vast shoals, particularly in the Southern Ocean and Antarctic waters, providing food for many animals. Baleen whales, such as the blue whale, swim through these shoals with their mouths open. When a whale's mouth is full, it squeezes the water out through special strainers and swallows the krill.

Migration

Everywhere on Earth, other than at the Equator, the climate is seasonal. This means that part of the year is too dry or cold for most plants to grow. But most animals must eat all year round. And their young need to be born in the right place and at the right time, so there will be enough food to feed them.

Many animals avoid difficult seasons by migrating. Each year, as the weather changes, and their food supply begins to run out, they make a journey to where the climate and food supply will enable them to survive. Some of these journeys are very long.

Key to migration routes

- Monarch butterfly
- Grey whale
- Caribou
- Eel
- Swallow
- Wildebeest
- Arctic tern

Grey whales move south in winter, away from the icy seas in the north

Each spring and autumn, monarch butterflies fly nearly 3,000 kilometres

Eels migrate to and from the Sargasso Sea

Arctic terns have the longest migration – twice a year they fly non-stop for four months to cover the 18,000 kilometres between the north and south poles

Seasons

The Earth takes a year to orbit the Sun and a day to turn on its own axis. This axis is not at right angles to the Sun's rays, so as the Earth orbits, first one hemisphere and then the other is tilted towards the Sun. This produces the seasons. The hemisphere facing the Sun experiences summer, while the other hemisphere has its winter.

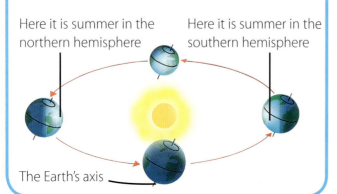

Here it is summer in the northern hemisphere

Here it is summer in the southern hemisphere

The Earth's axis

North American caribou spend summer in the tundra, then travel 800 kilometres south to conifer forests

Eels from rivers in Europe and America migrate to the Sargasso Sea to breed

Seasons and the tundra

In winter, there is little food in the frozen lands called the tundra (1). Reindeer scratch through the snow to find food, but most animals leave to seek warmer conditions.

Plants grow rapidly during the tundra's brief summer (2). Insects, too, breed and swarm in the ponds and marshes. For a while, food is abundant and many birds and animals arrive to feed.

European swallows migrate to Africa for the winter

In the savannah dry season, wildebeest travel 320 kilometres from the Serengeti plain to Lake Victoria

23

Niches

Where there is anything a living organism can eat or digest and where there is shelter or enough space, sooner or later organisms will appear that will put these resources to use. The new arrival may be a plant, an animal or a colony of bacteria. Once settled in its home, the organism has created a 'niche', a place within the larger community of living things.

Find a stone that has been on the ground undisturbed for a long time and you may see lichen or moss growing on it. It has found a place to attach itself, from where it can obtain the food it needs and get enough water from the moist air or rain. It has found its niche and, in doing so, it also provides niches for others, including the tiny animals that feed on it. On a single oak tree (*right*), there may be hundreds of niches.

Oak host

Gall wasps (**1**) lay their eggs on the buds of oak trees. When the larvae hatch, they produce chemicals that cause apple-like swellings called 'galls' (**2**). These protect the larvae and provide food for them while they grow.

The woodpecker's nest

A woodpecker drills into the bark to find insects

A moth, with markings that make it almost invisible, rests on a patch of lichen

Lichens, fungi and ferns use the tree's branches and trunk to support them

Squirrels eat acorns and nest high above the ground, where they are safe

Bank voles find food and shelter in the grass around tree roots

Caterpillars feed on the tree's leaves

A niche for a beetle

An oak tree shelters and feeds many insects and their young. The grubs of longhorn beetles eat the wood, drilling tunnels as they chew. If there are too many of them, the tree can be seriously harmed.

Bats may roost in holes in the tree

The tawny owl rests in the tree, watching and listening for its prey

Many songbirds, such as this blackbird, sleep and build nests among branches

Urban niche

Foxes eat almost anything. Though their natural habitat is in the countryside, many can now be found in urban areas, where there is a plentiful supply of waste human food. Our parks and gardens provide shelter for them, and our dustbins supply food, so foxes have made a niche for themselves near our homes.

Food and water for plant life collect in hollows and crevices in the bark

Some tiny wasps make the tree grow galls in which they shelter their young

Rivers

When rainwater falls on bare rock or thin soil, it flows downhill across the surface of the land. If the soil is deep, the rainwater first soaks downwards until it meets rock before it flows downhill. This underground water is called groundwater. In hollows, where the rock layer is close to the surface, it may form a natural spring.

On the surface of the land, water flows along channels. A small channel of water is called a stream. The water wears away at the channel, making it deeper. As more water joins the channel from high ground or springs, the tiny stream grows into a river. Rivers are home to many plants and animals, which typically live in distinct zones. These zones are often named after the fish species usually found there.

Minnow zone

The river slows as it leaves the hills. Sediment (mud) collects on the stony bottom and plants take root in it. This is the minnow, or grayling, zone. Minnows and graylings feed on small animals such as young fish and insects.

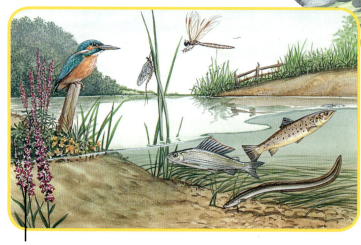

Plants take root in the river sediment

On almost level ground, the river meanders (its path twists from side to side)

The land is nearly flat here – it is called the flood plain

The river flows out to sea

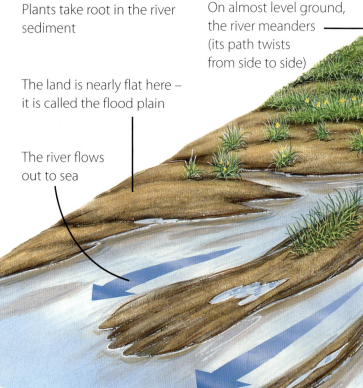

Sediment builds up into a mudbank

Estuary zone

An estuary is where a river widens and meets the sea. The incoming tide brings salty sea water upstream. Where the sea and river waters mix, tiny particles sink to form mudbanks, where the sea may deposit sand. Worms and other small animals feed in the mud. They in turn are food for wading birds. The heron hunts for fish in the shallow water (*below*).

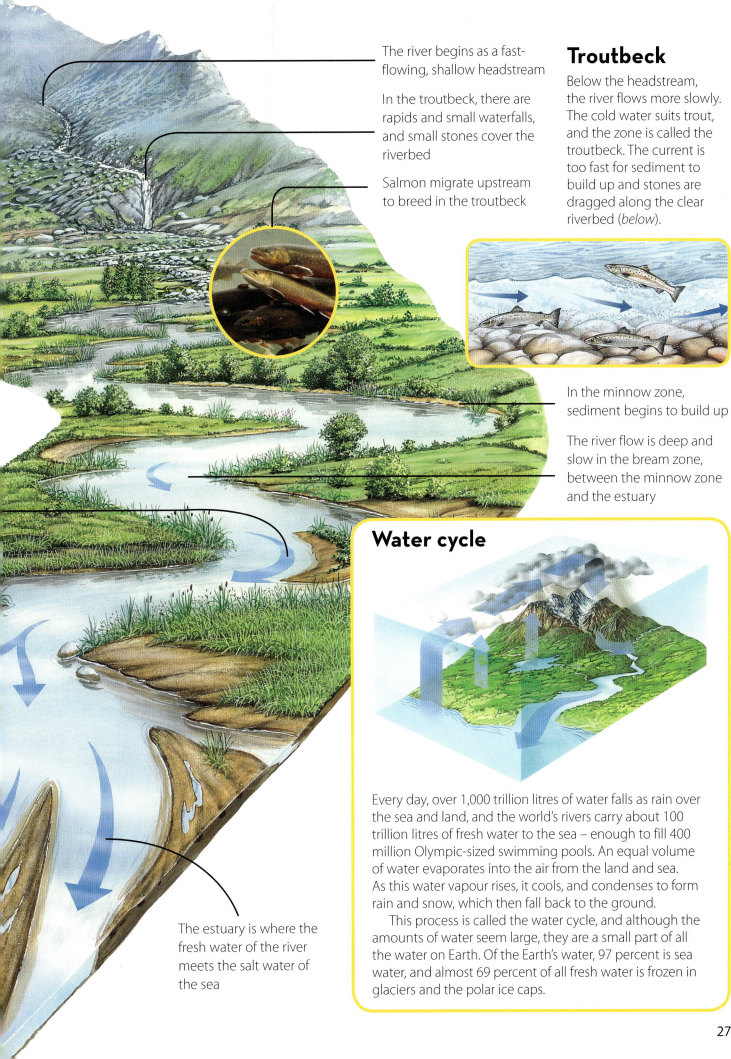

The river begins as a fast-flowing, shallow headstream

In the troutbeck, there are rapids and small waterfalls, and small stones cover the riverbed

Salmon migrate upstream to breed in the troutbeck

Troutbeck

Below the headstream, the river flows more slowly. The cold water suits trout, and the zone is called the troutbeck. The current is too fast for sediment to build up and stones are dragged along the clear riverbed (*below*).

In the minnow zone, sediment begins to build up

The river flow is deep and slow in the bream zone, between the minnow zone and the estuary

Water cycle

Every day, over 1,000 trillion litres of water falls as rain over the sea and land, and the world's rivers carry about 100 trillion litres of fresh water to the sea – enough to fill 400 million Olympic-sized swimming pools. An equal volume of water evaporates into the air from the land and sea. As this water vapour rises, it cools, and condenses to form rain and snow, which then fall back to the ground.

This process is called the water cycle, and although the amounts of water seem large, they are a small part of all the water on Earth. Of the Earth's water, 97 percent is sea water, and almost 69 percent of all fresh water is frozen in glaciers and the polar ice caps.

The estuary is where the fresh water of the river meets the salt water of the sea

Ecosystems

An ecosystem is a community of plants and animals that live together, drawing on the same food and energy sources from their surroundings. If one community is different from others nearby, it can be studied by itself as an ecosystem.

Tropical rainforests are very rich ecosystems. They grow near the Equator, where the climate is hot and wet. They can support many more kinds of plants and animals than habitats in cooler climates, because plants grow rapidly and there is no cold or dry season to slow or interrupt their growth. On this page, we see how rainforests provide countless niches and many small ecosystems within the main rainforest ecosystem.

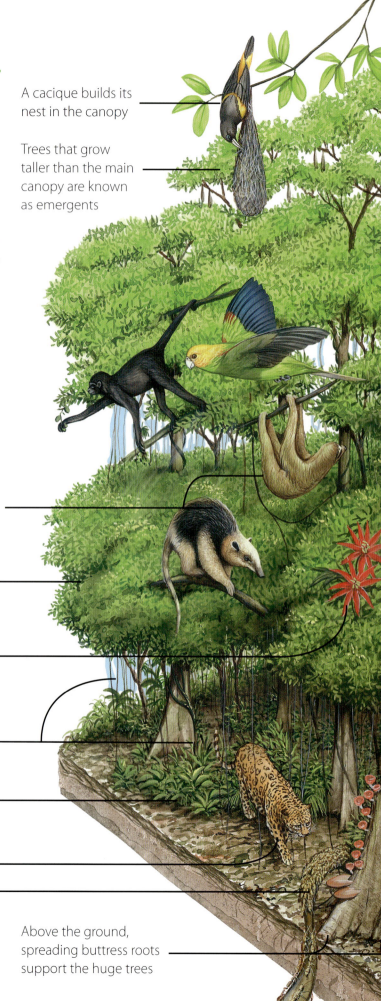

A cacique builds its nest in the canopy

Trees that grow taller than the main canopy are known as emergents

The tamandua and sloth live in the canopy (treetops), where there is more food, such as fruit and insects

Young trees form a lower canopy

Epiphytes are plants, often rootless, that grow on trees – this is a bromeliad

Lianas are climbers that grow up trees towards the light – they hang like ropes from the branches

Saplings and shrubs grow on the shady forest floor

A jaguar hunts for its prey on the dark forest floor

An army of ants

Above the ground, spreading buttress roots support the huge trees

Birds such as this parrot have strong beaks for cracking nuts

A harpy eagle preys on monkeys and other tree-dwellers

Toucans eat fruit, insects and lizards

Forest birds

Hummingbirds hover among the trees in the forest canopy, taking nectar from flowers like orchids. In moving from flower to flower, they spread pollen so that the flowers produce seeds. Other birds, such as macaws and toucans, also enjoy the fruits of plants and trees. Birds help to spread the seeds of plants by passing them out as waste after digesting the fruit they eat.

Branches act as a road network for hunters like the ocelot

A spider preys on a tree frog

The boa constrictor waits for a squirrel or other small mammal

The agouti listens for falling fruit, which it then eats

The katydid – this insect disguises itself as a dead leaf

The forest floor

The dark, damp forest floor forms an ecosystem of its own. Plant eaters and meat eaters live there, like the fruit-eating agouti and the hunting jaguar. Smaller animals and insects break up the fallen leaves. This helps the dead matter to decompose, recycling its nutrients within the ecosystem. Leafcutter ants (*right*) shred huge amounts of vegetation. They cut up fallen leaves and take the pieces to underground nests. They eat the fungus that then grows on the leaf pieces.

Biomes

When one type of ecosystem covers a vast area, it is called a biome. Different climates produce different biomes. There are many biomes in Africa, including tropical rainforest, savannah grassland and desert. A desert biome, such as the Sahara in northern Africa, forms where there is little rain. Here, temperatures run to extremes, so it can be freezing at night after being scorchingly hot during the day. Bordering the Sahara desert are savannah grasslands, which are also warm and dry, but, unlike the deserts, heavy rains fall here in late spring.

In the Sahara, daytime temperatures are around 40°C

Less than 5 cm of rain falls each year in some parts of the Sahara

Sandstorms occur when strong winds lift dust and sand high into the air

Fennec Fox

Jerboa

Biomes map

- Mixed forest
- Mountain
- Grassland
- Tropical rainforest
- Semi-desert
- Desert

The Sahara has vast sand seas called ergs, but in parts the land is rocky

Plants with long roots find water deep underground

Camels can survive without water for more than two weeks

Desert soil is thin

Desert animals

Animals have adapted to the desert climate. Lizards and jerboa shelter from the heat in burrows. The fennec fox and jerboa (*see above*) have large ears that are rich in blood vessels, which helps them lose body heat. Ostriches can drink the desert's salty water and do not suffer if their body temperature rises.

50–200 cm of rain falls each year in the savannah

In the savannah, daytime temperatures are around 20°C

In the dry season, grassland fires are common

After the fire

Fires are common in the dry savannah. Plants and trees are destroyed, but seeds survive, as they lie hidden deep in the soil. The topsoil is enriched by ash from the fire and by the decomposed remains of plants.

Seeds survive below the surface of the soil

Grassland grazers

Grazing animals live in large herds. Each type of animal prefers different plants, so they do not fight over their food. In the dry season, when water is scarce, animals meet at waterholes. Elephants, wildebeest, zebras, giraffes and others drink or wallow together peacefully. But the animals must remain alert because the waterhole also attracts hunters, such as lions, leopards, cheetahs and hyenas. Some grassland animals, like the impala, get all their water from dew-soaked grass, so they do not need to drink at waterholes.

As the dry season approaches, mixed herds of grazers migrate to find fresh pasture

Trees like the baobab resist drought and grow rapidly during the rainy season

The savannah is a region of tall grasses and scattered trees that turns green only when it rains

Waterholes form in hollows, where underground water seeps to the surface

Savannah soil is deeper than desert soil

Elephants gather at the waterhole

Nutrient Cycles

All living things, including people, are made of about 20 chemical elements, including carbon, nitrogen, calcium and sulphur. Plants and animals use these nutrients to build their cells and to provide energy, and must regularly top them up. The nutrients come from the environment. Plants absorb water and dissolved mineral nutrients such as sulphur and calcium from the soil. They absorb carbon from the air. Animals take in their nutrients by eating plants or other animals.

All nutrients follow cycles and are eventually returned to the environment, so new living things can live and grow. If nutrients did not move through cycles, soon there would be none left and all life would cease.

The sulphur cycle

This illustration shows how the nutrient sulphur follows a cycle. Dissolved sulphur from rocks is taken up by plants, and passes to animals that eat the plants. As animal waste and dead animal and plant matter decompose, sulphur is returned to the ground. Here, it is washed away by groundwater and rivers to the sea. Some sulphur is trapped in mud in estuaries, where bacteria release it in a different form back into the air. Most of the sulphur that reaches the sea is taken in by tiny plants called plankton. These also release the sulphur back into the air. Sulphur compounds in the air dissolve in rain, and eventually fall back to the ground, where the cycle begins again.

Volcanoes also release sulphur from beneath the Earth's crust into the air. They return some of the sulphur that is trapped deep underground to the sulphur cycle.

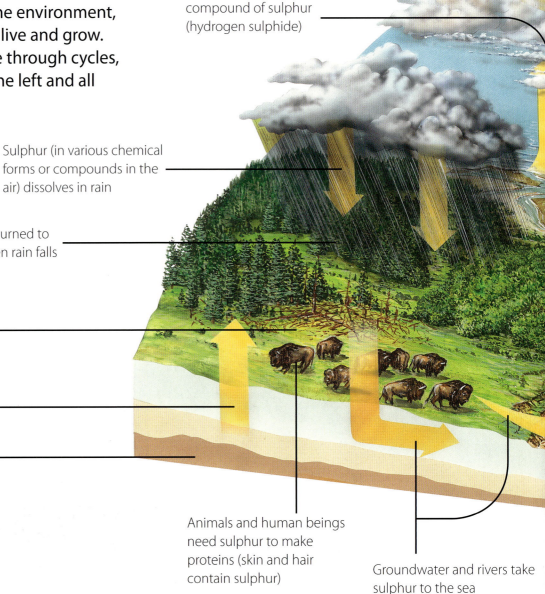

Bacteria living in mud and marshes release a compound of sulphur (hydrogen sulphide)

Sulphur (in various chemical forms or compounds in the air) dissolves in rain

Sulphur is returned to the land when rain falls

Nutrients in dead plants and animals are released back into the ground as they decompose

Sulphur is taken up by living plants and animals

Sulphur originally comes from rock

Animals and human beings need sulphur to make proteins (skin and hair contain sulphur)

Groundwater and rivers take sulphur to the sea

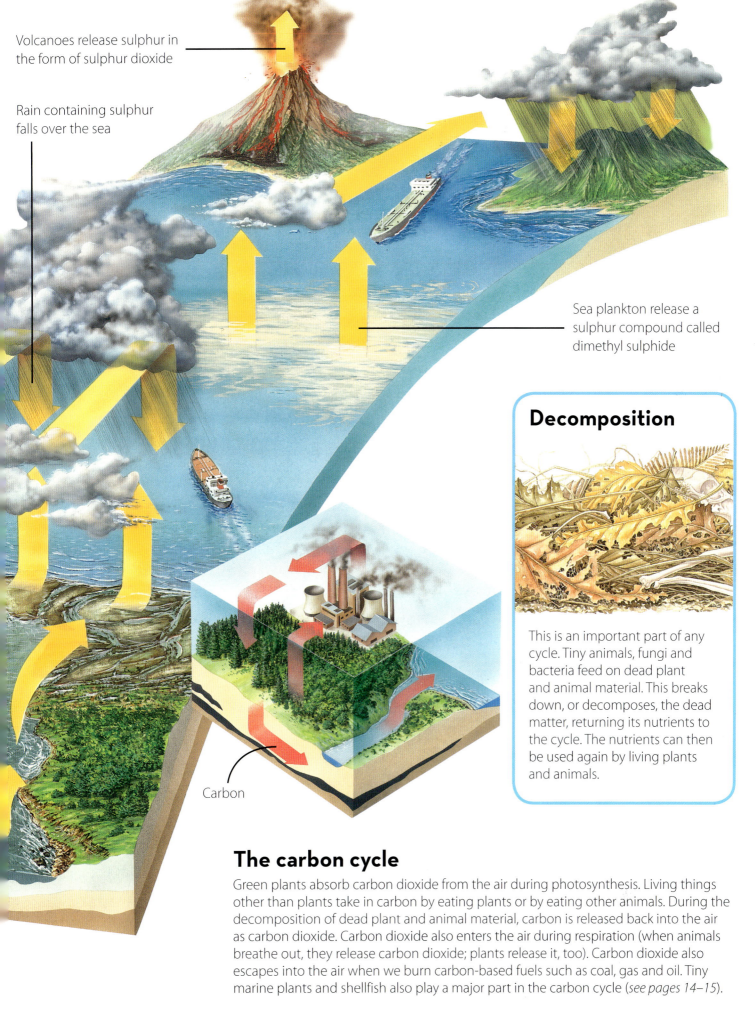

Volcanoes release sulphur in the form of sulphur dioxide

Rain containing sulphur falls over the sea

Sea plankton release a sulphur compound called dimethyl sulphide

Carbon

Decomposition

This is an important part of any cycle. Tiny animals, fungi and bacteria feed on dead plant and animal material. This breaks down, or decomposes, the dead matter, returning its nutrients to the cycle. The nutrients can then be used again by living plants and animals.

The carbon cycle

Green plants absorb carbon dioxide from the air during photosynthesis. Living things other than plants take in carbon by eating plants or by eating other animals. During the decomposition of dead plant and animal material, carbon is released back into the air as carbon dioxide. Carbon dioxide also enters the air during respiration (when animals breathe out, they release carbon dioxide; plants release it, too). Carbon dioxide also escapes into the air when we burn carbon-based fuels such as coal, gas and oil. Tiny marine plants and shellfish also play a major part in the carbon cycle (*see pages 14–15*).

Obtaining Nitrogen

A nutrient cycle involves many complicated chemical changes. This is especially true of the nitrogen cycle. Although there is plenty of nitrogen in the air, there is a problem. Plants and animals cannot use nitrogen as a gas: it must be in the form of food. This means the gas has to be changed into nitrogen compounds, such as nitrates. Bacteria in the soil do this complicated job. They change nitrogen into nitrates, which plants can then use to make proteins (the chemical 'building blocks' from which plant and animal bodies are made). Later in the cycle, animals take in the nitrates when they eat the plants.

The air is mostly nitrogen gas

Energy from lightning changes nitrogen gas into a compound that dissolves in water

Nitrogen compounds fall to the ground in rainwater

Nitrates in water enter plant roots and feed the plant

Nitrogen cycle

Nitrates in moisture in the soil are drawn up through the roots of plants. The plants use the nitrates to make proteins. Animals that eat the plants change the plant proteins into animal proteins.

Animal and plant waste contains proteins and other nitrogen compounds. So when they decompose, the nitrogen compounds are once more available to plants. Some bacteria, called denitrifying bacteria, break down nitrogen compounds and release nitrogen gas back into the air.

Denitrifying bacteria

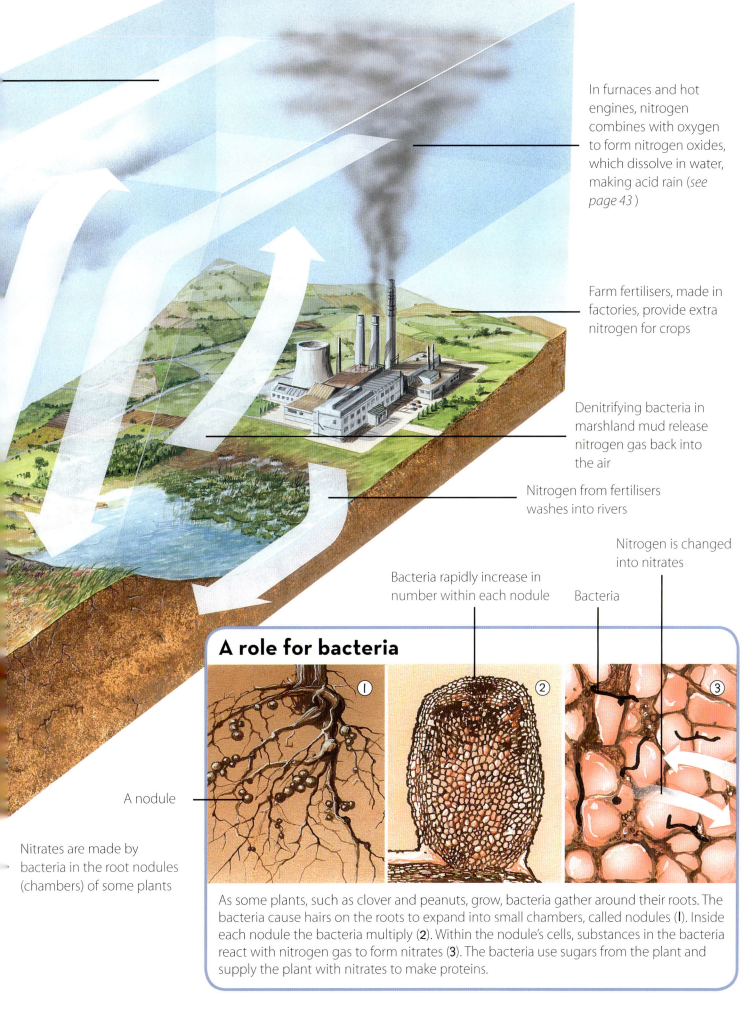

In furnaces and hot engines, nitrogen combines with oxygen to form nitrogen oxides, which dissolve in water, making acid rain (*see page 43*)

Farm fertilisers, made in factories, provide extra nitrogen for crops

Denitrifying bacteria in marshland mud release nitrogen gas back into the air

Nitrogen from fertilisers washes into rivers

Nitrogen is changed into nitrates

Bacteria rapidly increase in number within each nodule

Bacteria

A role for bacteria

A nodule

Nitrates are made by bacteria in the root nodules (chambers) of some plants

As some plants, such as clover and peanuts, grow, bacteria gather around their roots. The bacteria cause hairs on the roots to expand into small chambers, called nodules (**1**). Inside each nodule the bacteria multiply (**2**). Within the nodule's cells, substances in the bacteria react with nitrogen gas to form nitrates (**3**). The bacteria use sugars from the plant and supply the plant with nitrates to make proteins.

Soil

Soil is made up of tiny pieces of rock and the decayed remains of dead organisms. The rock fragments have been created after thousands of years of weathering. Near the surface of the land, the heat of summer makes rocks expand and the cold of winter makes them shrink. This causes the rocks to crack and rainwater then trickles into the cracks. In winter, the water freezes and expands, widening the cracks and causing fragments of rock to break off. Acids in the water also weaken the rock so that it breaks apart more easily. Rocks deeper underground are weakened by water that seeps up from below. All these processes, called weathering, help to make soil by breaking up the rock.

The type of soil varies according to the rock from which it forms – it can be light and sandy or heavy and clay-like

Water moves between the particles of soil

Water in soil

Rainwater moves down from the Earth's surface between rock particles until it can go no further. This underground water is called groundwater and its upper surface is called the water table. As water dries, or evaporates, on the surface of the soil, it is replaced by groundwater, drawn upwards through very small gaps. This upward movement of water keeps the soil moist.

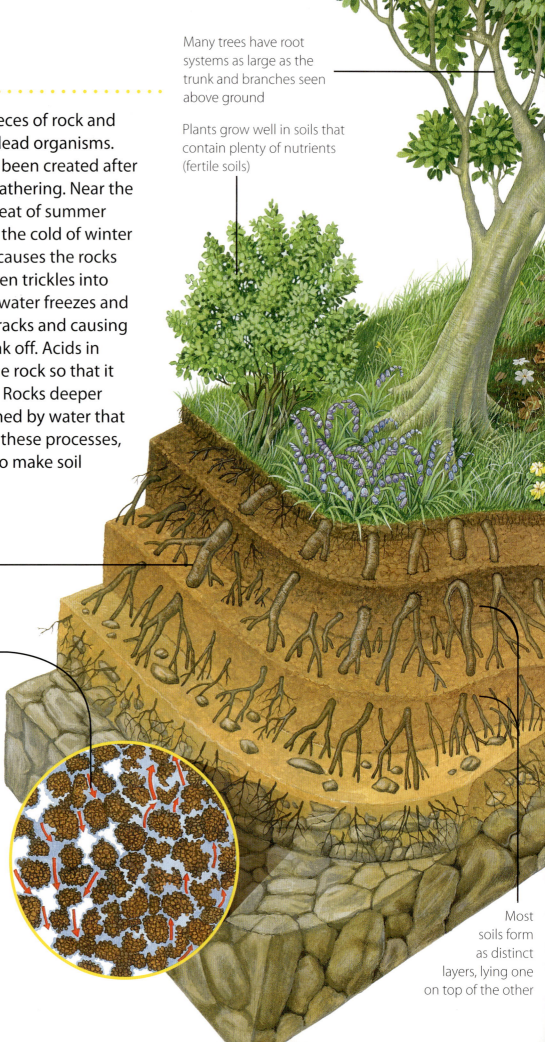

Many trees have root systems as large as the trunk and branches seen above ground

Plants grow well in soils that contain plenty of nutrients (fertile soils)

Most soils form as distinct layers, lying one on top of the other

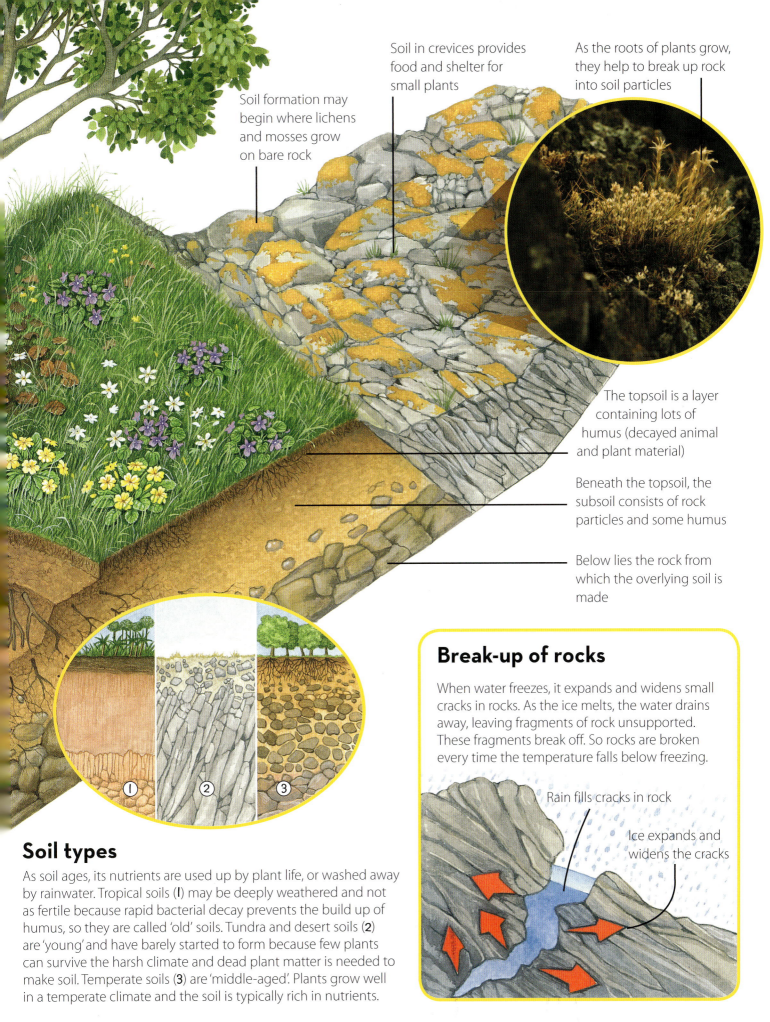

Soil formation may begin where lichens and mosses grow on bare rock

Soil in crevices provides food and shelter for small plants

As the roots of plants grow, they help to break up rock into soil particles

The topsoil is a layer containing lots of humus (decayed animal and plant material)

Beneath the topsoil, the subsoil consists of rock particles and some humus

Below lies the rock from which the overlying soil is made

Break-up of rocks

When water freezes, it expands and widens small cracks in rocks. As the ice melts, the water drains away, leaving fragments of rock unsupported. These fragments break off. So rocks are broken every time the temperature falls below freezing.

Rain fills cracks in rock

Ice expands and widens the cracks

Soil types

As soil ages, its nutrients are used up by plant life, or washed away by rainwater. Tropical soils (1) may be deeply weathered and not as fertile because rapid bacterial decay prevents the build up of humus, so they are called 'old' soils. Tundra and desert soils (2) are 'young' and have barely started to form because few plants can survive the harsh climate and dead plant matter is needed to make soil. Temperate soils (3) are 'middle-aged'. Plants grow well in a temperate climate and the soil is typically rich in nutrients.

Soil Life

The organisms living in the top few centimetres of soil in a field of grass may weigh more than the cows grazing the pasture. A fertile soil teems with life, from single-celled bacteria to animals such as moles. Each organism occupies its own niche within the soil ecosystem. Woodlice, for example, eat decaying plant matter and their droppings provide tiny particles of simpler food for smaller organisms.

By living in or on the surface of the soil, organisms actually help to make more soil. They do this by eating and breaking down animal and plant material.

Mites

There are more mites than any other type of soil animal. Mites are tiny relatives of spiders. Plant-eating mites break leaves into smaller pieces (*below*). Other mites hunt animals such as nematodes.

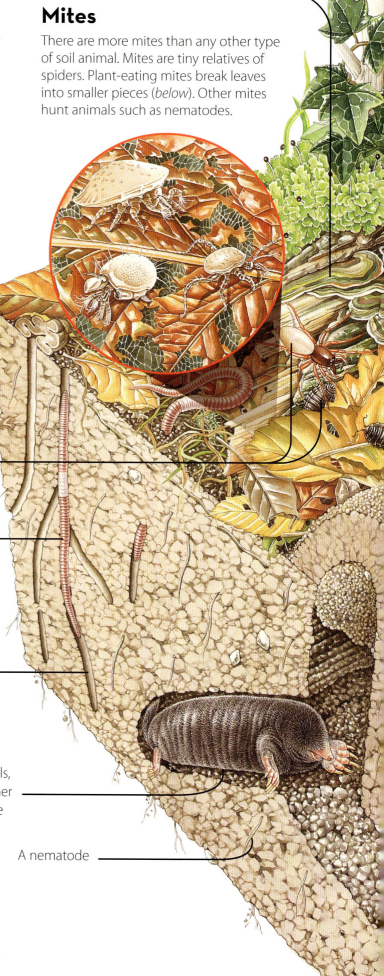

Fungi break down wood

Nematodes

There are a vast number of nematodes (eelworms) in the soil. There may be a million of them living in the first 10 centimetres below a square metre of the surface. They are thread-like and the largest are barely 2 millimetres long. They live in water in the soil and eat other nematodes or single-celled organisms such as bacteria. Nematodes help to control the size of the microscopic soil population.

A spider hunts for lice

Earthworms tunnel to the surface at night to deposit their casts (waste matter)

Worm tunnels create space for air to circulate through the soil

The mole digs long tunnels, eating the worms and other small animals it finds there

A nematode

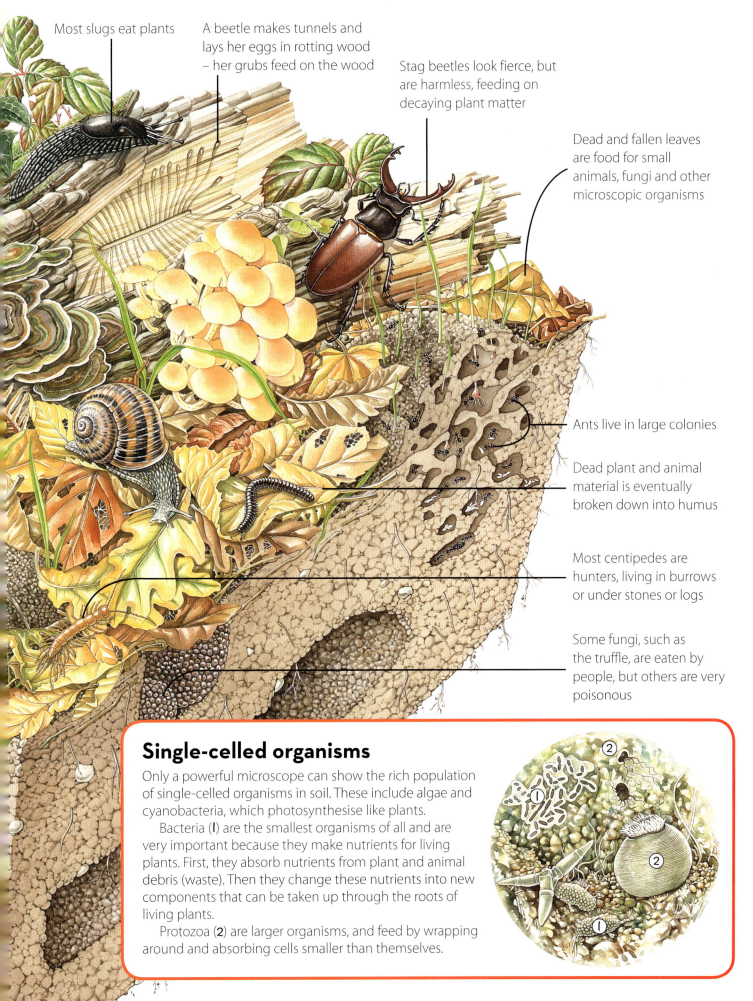

Most slugs eat plants

A beetle makes tunnels and lays her eggs in rotting wood – her grubs feed on the wood

Stag beetles look fierce, but are harmless, feeding on decaying plant matter

Dead and fallen leaves are food for small animals, fungi and other microscopic organisms

Ants live in large colonies

Dead plant and animal material is eventually broken down into humus

Most centipedes are hunters, living in burrows or under stones or logs

Some fungi, such as the truffle, are eaten by people, but others are very poisonous

Single-celled organisms

Only a powerful microscope can show the rich population of single-celled organisms in soil. These include algae and cyanobacteria, which photosynthesise like plants.

Bacteria (**1**) are the smallest organisms of all and are very important because they make nutrients for living plants. First, they absorb nutrients from plant and animal debris (waste). Then they change these nutrients into new components that can be taken up through the roots of living plants.

Protozoa (**2**) are larger organisms, and feed by wrapping around and absorbing cells smaller than themselves.

Energy

Energy is the capacity to do work. Factories use energy to drive the machines that make goods to be sold around the world in shops and online. We use energy at home to cook our meals, provide light, power our TVs and computers, heat water and to keep us warm in winter and cool when it's hot. Road, rail, sea and air transport also use energy.

Currently, much of our energy comes from fossil fuels – coal, oil and natural gas – but these resources are not unlimited and can contribute to climate change. We need to use more renewable energy sources, such as solar and wind energy, to generate power.

Renewable energy

Dams (*below left*) contain turbines that are worked by the flow of water to generate hydroelectric power. The ebb and flow of tides and the movement of sea waves can also drive turbines. Wind turbines (*below right*) convert wind energy to electricity. Energy from sunlight can be converted directly to electricity, or used to raise steam to drive generators, when focused with mirrors. These technologies release no carbon dioxide (CO_2), but hydroelectric and tidal sites are limited, and wind power is not always popular due to the visual impact of turbines on the landscape, and they can pose a threat to wildlife and their habitats.

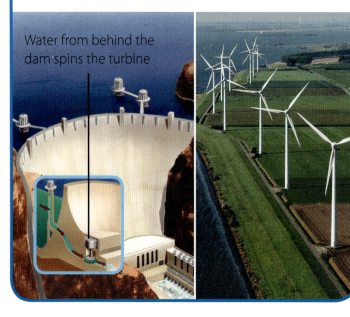

Water from behind the dam spins the turbine

Air pollution

Burning fuel generates heat, but it also produces ash, smoke and polluting gases. To reduce pollution, power stations and factories must capture these pollutants and dispose of them safely. Fires also produce carbon dioxide (CO_2), which builds up in the air. Many scientists believe this is making the world's climate grow warmer and that we should find ways to release less CO_2.

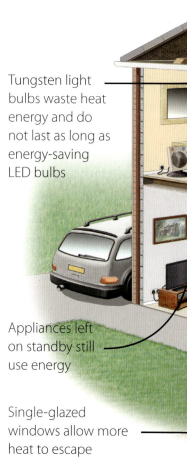

An uninsulated roof allows up to 30 percent of household heat to escape into the atmosphere

Unlagged water tanks

Tungsten light bulbs waste heat energy and do not last as long as energy-saving LED bulbs

Appliances left on standby still use energy

Single-glazed windows allow more heat to escape

Transport

Trains and trams can run on electricity from overhead or trackside lines, but other forms of transport must carry their fuel or power source with them. Electric cars are becoming more widely used around the world, especially in cities, and fuel-cell cars are being developed that will oxidise hydrogen to generate power. Modern aircraft designs are more fuel-efficient, but reducing the amount of flying is the most effective way to cut carbon emissions from aviation.

Improving efficiency

Modern domestic appliances and energy-saving light bulbs are designed to reduce electricity use, but we can also save energy by switching off appliances that are not being used and turning down the central heating thermostat. Saving energy also reduces costs. The cutaway picture below compares an energy-inefficient home (*below left*) with a more modern energy-efficient equilvalent (*below*).

Solar panels can provide hot water or electricity

Domestic wind turbines can be used to generate electricity, so reducing household energy bills

Heat loss from hot water tanks is minimsed by foam insulation

Nuclear energy

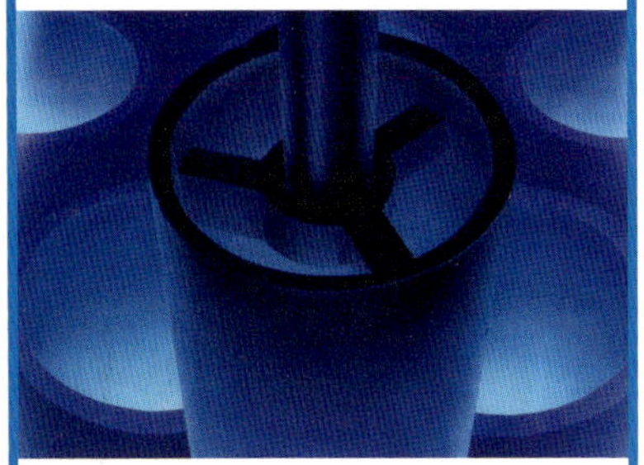

Nuclear reactors produce electricity efficiently and release no carbon dioxide, but cannot respond to sudden demand peaks. They also produce radioactive waste that requires careful disposal.

Showering uses up to a third less water than a having a bath

Digital controls and thermostatic radiator valves match heating to needs

A ground source heat pump, buried in a trench, can provide heating or hot water

A water butt collects rainwater for reuse

Cavity wall insulation

Energy-efficient boiler for hot water and heating

Double-glazed windows reduce conductive heat loss (through the glass) and minimise draughts

Energy-efficient appliances

Biofuels

Some plant crops are grown specifically for use as fuel. Biofuels will not run out, but the crops occupy land that could otherwise be used to grow food. This increases food prices. Alternatively, they can be grown in areas not previously cultivated, but this can destroy the habitats of other plants and animals.

Environmental Damage

We cannot avoid altering our environment, and many of the changes we make are beneficial. But a lot of human activities do harm the environment. Clearing rainforests or other natural vegetation to make farmland reduces animal and plant habitats. The plants and animals become confined to smaller and smaller areas and some species can die out altogether. Waste products from our homes and factories can pollute the air, oceans and rivers. Pollution can poison organisms directly, or indirectly by damaging their environment.

Conservation

Golden lion tamarins are tree dwellers in the tropical forests of South America. When trees are felled, there is nowhere for them to live. In 1971, there were fewer than 200 left in the wild, so a conservation program began. As a result, there are now more than 1,000 living in the wild in the Brazilian forest, but they are still classified as endangered.

Trees are essential to the environment – they use up carbon dioxide and provide oxygen and water vapour

About 46,000 square kilometres of tropical rainforest are cleared each year (an area bigger than Switzerland)

Vegetation that cannot be used is burned once the useful timber has been removed

Forest is cleared to allow mining for minerals

Once roads are built, farmers and multinational companies move into the forest and clear more land to grow crops

The soil is poor and crops often fail

In some places, cleared ground becomes as hard as concrete

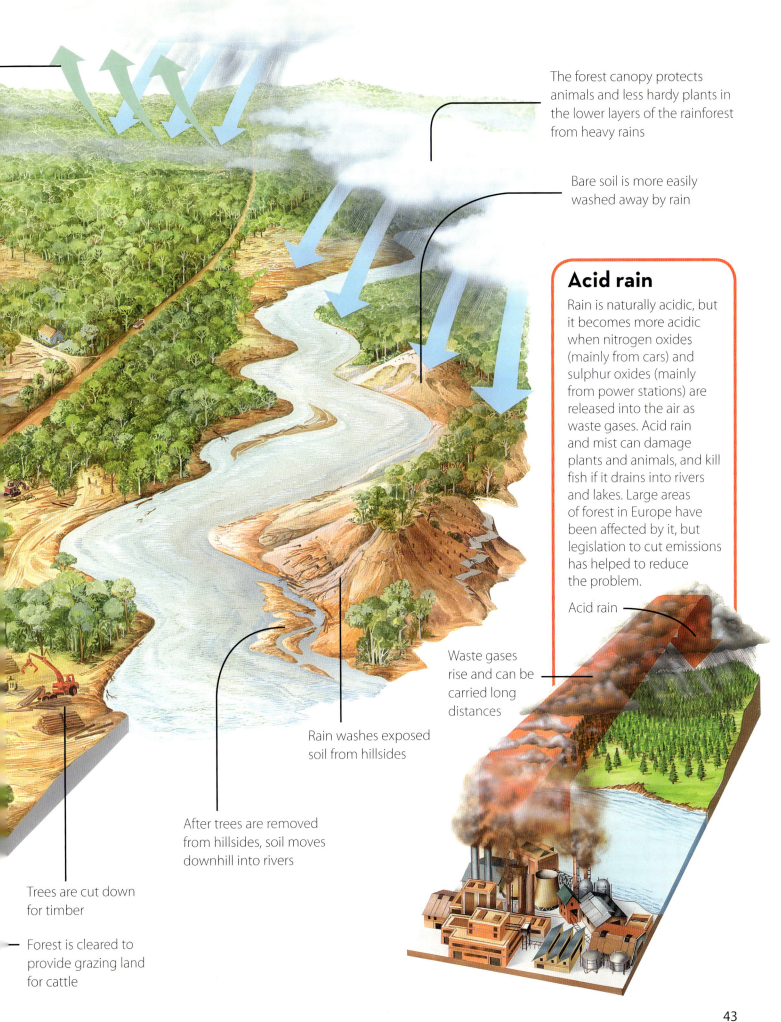

The forest canopy protects animals and less hardy plants in the lower layers of the rainforest from heavy rains

Bare soil is more easily washed away by rain

Acid rain

Rain is naturally acidic, but it becomes more acidic when nitrogen oxides (mainly from cars) and sulphur oxides (mainly from power stations) are released into the air as waste gases. Acid rain and mist can damage plants and animals, and kill fish if it drains into rivers and lakes. Large areas of forest in Europe have been affected by it, but legislation to cut emissions has helped to reduce the problem.

Acid rain

Waste gases rise and can be carried long distances

Rain washes exposed soil from hillsides

After trees are removed from hillsides, soil moves downhill into rivers

Trees are cut down for timber

Forest is cleared to provide grazing land for cattle

43

Learning to Live in Harmony

Today, many large industrial companies take care to cause as little environmental damage as possible. Some are working to restore areas that were damaged in the past. Mines, such as the china clay mine seen below, can destroy wildlife and result in large waste tips. For every tonne of china clay taken out of the land, there are nine tonnes of waste. But even the large waste tips from a china clay mine can be transformed. Once the mining has finished, the area can be landscaped and replanted to create a leisure facility, such as a playing field or golf course. The hills may be used as grazing land for sheep. The illustrations on these pages show how this is done.

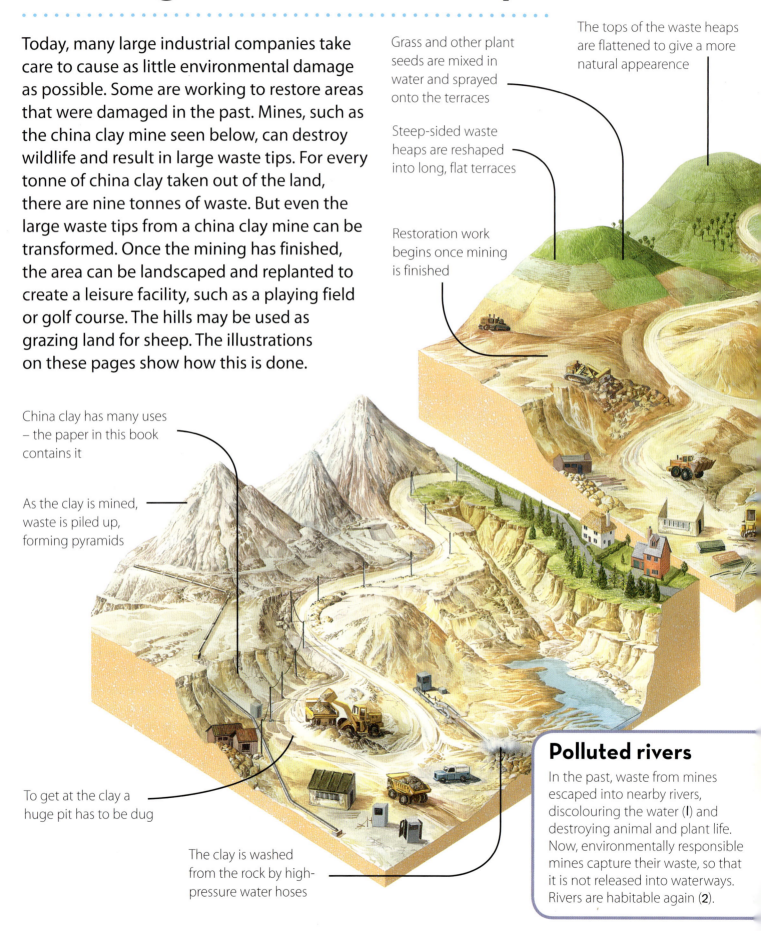

Grass and other plant seeds are mixed in water and sprayed onto the terraces

The tops of the waste heaps are flattened to give a more natural appearence

Steep-sided waste heaps are reshaped into long, flat terraces

Restoration work begins once mining is finished

China clay has many uses – the paper in this book contains it

As the clay is mined, waste is piled up, forming pyramids

To get at the clay a huge pit has to be dug

The clay is washed from the rock by high-pressure water hoses

Polluted rivers

In the past, waste from mines escaped into nearby rivers, discolouring the water (I) and destroying animal and plant life. Now, environmentally responsible mines capture their waste, so that it is not released into waterways. Rivers are habitable again (2).

Recycling

Burying rubbish in landfill sites is costly and wasteful. Recycling glass, metals, some plastics, paper and card, cloth and other materials reduces the demand for raw materials and the amount of waste sent to landfill.

Large machines reshape the landscape

Alaska pipeline

In Alaska, a pipeline was needed to carry oil and gas from the north to the south. Because it crossed the caribou migration route (*see pages 22–23*), it was built on stilts so caribou could pass underneath. Raising the pipe also stopped it from melting the frozen soil. Damage to the frozen soil would affect the area's wildlife.

Putting vegetation back

Nitrate-producing plants, such as clover (*below*), are included in seed mixtures to put nitrogen back into the soil. Alder trees can be planted to help remove surplus water. While mining is in progress, waste material can be used to build large banks. Trees can be grown on the banks to hide the mine and shield the surroundings from the dust.

Mining companies now try to leave the land restored or suitable for new uses

A lake can attract new wildlife, such as birds and insects

Water-filled pits are turned into lakes for recreation

②

The reclaimed land can be put to many uses, such as a golf course, or a nature reserve

Usage and recovery

Many items that are of no further use can be 'repurposed' and reused. Waste water is purified and returned to the supply. Fleece material for clothing can be made from plastic bottles. Old tyres can be turned into flooring, a safe surface for playgrounds, or even fuel. Food waste and paper make good compost that enriches soil and helps plants to grow.

Index